Finding Your Voice

Emotional expression through creativity

SARAH FREED

Lulu Press Inc, North Carolina, United States. 2018

Lulu Press Inc
627 Davis Drive
Suite 300
Morrisville
North Carolina 27560
United States
www.lulu.com

ISBN: 978-0-244-99646-8

Sarah Freed is a Counsellor, Psychotherapist, Couples Therapist and Creative Arts Therapist working in private practice near Cambridge, UK.

She is the author of Mending the Soul, A Journey Beyond Abuse, Lulu Publishing, 2017

For more information visit her website at www.cambstherapy.org

To Sharone, April and Nathan. With you, I have learnt what love is.

Contents

Introduction

In *Finding Your Voice* I offer to you a selection of poetry that has been written over six years. It brings together my observations of life through the lens of feelings and shows how the stirring of the psyche can lead to a greater sense of identity. My intention in offering up my experience to you, the reader, is to share with you how creativity has helped me to heal the old wounds of the past. My personal story is inextricably connected with my professional life. I have been a counsellor and psychotherapist working with adults and couples for over fifteen years and, as such, have learnt an invaluable amount about human nature along the way. Up until two years ago, I offered talking therapy only, but my introduction to the use of creative arts in the therapeutic environment totally transformed my work. It also helped me massively on a personal level. I now use materials such as clay, the sand tray, pens, pastels and crayons, play dough, shells and stones to enable people to express their experiences. I have discovered that, often, talking only takes the healing so far and words can act as a form of avoidance of feelings.

This book is also my way of attempting to present some of the key things I've learnt during my time as a therapist about the human condition, in an accessible, easy to understand way. I have read countless therapy-type books over the years but many of them have left me cold; not really understanding what the author is trying to convey. Their analytical explanations often have the tendency to go over my head! The beauty of working creatively, is that it is an experiential way of learning about yourself. Generally, we all really just want to make sense of our own experience.

We all have wounds, in some shape or form, difficult things that have happened to us. A perfect upbringing doesn't exist. In the field of psychology, there is a commonly held view that all childhoods are traumatic. It's because of the huge amount of variances that can influence childhood which makes it completely unique. Even if you have siblings, with the same parents and same family set-up, they will have experienced childhood differently to you. Imagine that each sibling is like a camera on a movie set, all set at slightly different angles, each providing a unique viewpoint. The influence of our parent/s or main caregiver/s (or lack of them) sets a template for all other relationships throughout our lives. If our attachment to them is a bit shaky, we will find it more difficult to establish secure relationships later in life, although this is not impossible. Our siblings (or lack of them), the family set-up generally, peers and friendships, behaviours of others towards us as children, our environment, social expectations and pressure (particularly these days in the form of social media), our abilities and 'dis'abilities. All these elements mould us into the person we become.

In my experience, I would say that the number one reason for people accessing therapy is because they are disconnected in some way. It may manifest itself in different ways; causing them difficulties such as depression, anxiety, work stress, troubled relationships etc. Therapists call this the 'presenting issue', the *initial reason* stated for seeking therapy. But, more often than not, once a person enters the therapy and trust is established, a different pathway begins to open up.

They begin to learn that what they are struggling with is a manifestation of their disconnection with *themselves*. They feel lonely, alienated, uncertain, restless, insecure and they lack meaning in their lives. They don't know who they are or what they want. They may feel that they have everything they need but are still not happy and they don't understand why. What they need is to reconnect to their inner-world of thoughts - and most importantly – *feelings*, in order to live a more fulfilling life. To learn who they are and what they want. When we reconnect internally, we are more able to connect externally, with others.

Creativity helps one get in touch with fragmented or suppressed thoughts, feelings, memories and experiences in an effort to bring them to consciousness where they can be more understood and, ultimately, assimilated into self-awareness where they can be of use. To take time out, to be quiet, to be still, to sculpt, to mold, to draw, to write, to play. All this can provide the space to bring clarity, compassion, empathy. A different perspective sometimes. And this can be extremely helpful in understanding yourself better.

Poetry has become the main vehicle through which I have learned to consolidate my own experiences, by acknowledging my emotional response to them. My poems are an expression of my inner-world, turned outwards, which enables me to see and gain perspective on my experience. To develop what we call in psychotherapeutic terms, the 'third person'. Another set of eyes, slightly removed, a different viewpoint if you will. We are driven unconsciously, as adults, to do the work that wasn't done in childhood, to make up for what was missing. In many cases, this is the acknowledgement and validation of our emotions that we didn't receive from our parents. As children, we learn everything from our external world and in order to acknowledge our own feelings, we need them to be acknowledged firstly by someone else – to have them reflected back. And our parents, generally speaking, are our main resource for this – or should be ideally.

So, this is often the part that many people start to feel uncomfortable with because they feel it is disloyal to 'blame' their parents for their shortcomings. But it's not about blaming, more about *understanding*. There are many reasons why parents fall short; they may not have had good relationships with their own parents and struggle to know how to be a good parent themselves; there may be financial, environmental, social or relationship difficulties when a child comes into their family; the child may have been an accident or born out of complicated circumstances; a parent may have mental health or physical difficulties. I could go on, but the point is, our story is completely unique. The more we understand the circumstances of our early life, the more we can empathize.

The bottom line is that the perfect parent does not exist. Donald Winnicott, psychologist, coined the phrase, 'the good enough parent', someone who does their best; has the best interests of their child at heart, but inevitably cannot give the child everything they need because of their own experiences. As parents, we mix together the aspects of how we were parented in an attempt to replicate the good stuff, whilst trying to avoid the ways we may have been raised that we didn't like or felt didn't do us much good. All parents do it. But equally, we all have 'blind spots', the parts of our experience that we are not consciously aware of. So, we repeat these anyway, not consciously knowing that we are repeating some of the 'bad stuff' too. Nowhere is this more apparent than in our relationships with others. Therapy helps us to develop more self-awareness, to make us more consciously aware of how others experience us, bring to our awareness unhelpful patterns of behaviour which can be detrimental to our lives. It forces us to take a good, long, honest look in the mirror and see ourselves for what we truly are. It is the path to enlightenment and understanding. This is why it takes such courage to seek therapy – and why so many people avoid it or belittle it.

The psyche is stirred by our experiences in life and, for me, poetry has become a voice to express them. The word 'psychology' comes from the Greek word 'psyche' which means 'soul'. When I learnt this, it put a completely different spin on the work I was doing in the therapy room. I wasn't just supporting people with their mental health, I was helping them with a crisis in their soul. So, I began to develop a more holistic approach to wellbeing, incorporating mental, emotional, physical and spiritual health. This was something the Eastern cultures, of course, had been recognising for thousands of years. Here in the West, we have lost our way, looking to medicine to 'cure us', or quick fixes like CBT *(Cognitive Behavioural Therapy)*. The key is to find balance.

Creativity can open up a doorway to the Self, our core, the fundamental part of who we are. It can help us to reconnect with our true, authentic identity and once we are reconnected, the world becomes a very different place. We feel more confident and self-assured. We banish the self-doubt and fear of failure; that we will be found out one day and exposed as a fraud. I struggled with this fear for many years. We can be ourselves without fear of judgement from others. It also reminds us how to play and have fun. It can be dull being an adult, serious and with responsibilities. Creativity can help you reconnect with your inner-child and, if you have children of your own, you will notice that you find it easier to relate to them and your relationships improve.

I can honestly say to you that I do not care how others see me, because I have come to accept myself. I appreciate that everyone is entitled to their own opinion and will project their own 'stuff' onto me, but I can now separate myself from this. Projection is another psychological term. It happens all the time in our interactions with others. I describe it as being like at the cinema where a movie is projected onto the big screen. We see only what is in front of us. Imagine that I am the movie and I am full of fear that people don't like me, I will then unconsciously project this onto the person I am interacting with, because I want to get rid of the uncomfortable feeling this gives me. That person then unconsciously takes on this projection and – lo and behold – feels that they don't like me. But, the projection actually belongs to me, not the other person. Through therapy, we can learn to become more consciously aware of our projections and then, to own them and take responsibility for them, so that they don't interfere with our communication with others. Once I have been able to recognise this, I am able to say to myself logically 'this person doesn't know me, so how can they not like me?'

Creativity is everywhere and comes in so many forms; it's not just about art. So, try and have an awareness of what speaks to you. Dance, music, art, sculpture, gardening, cooking, sewing, building anything...the list is endless. Some of these things you probably do already without realising you are being creative. And you don't have to just stick with one form. Dance, music and movement are extremely important in my life as forms of expression. I have always loved music and singing and have learned that my early music tastes, for example, George Michael and Whitney Houston, were speaking to me on a very emotional level as a young person. In my world, there wasn't emotional validation or acknowledgement, but when I listen to those two artists now, I can see how their lyrics and vocals portrayed deeply emotional and troubled lives. At some level, this resonated with me, as I struggled to assimilate my own troubling experiences of childhood abuse and the resulting disconnection with myself and those close to me.

I've always exercised in some way and as a child and young person, I loved to dance. But in my 40s, I started doing Zumba classes and found a new way to express myself! Zumba, if you're not familiar with it, is a form of aerobic exercise set to Latin American style music. When the music starts, my body just *responds,* and I start to move! My hips sway, everything jiggles (but I don't care, I am in my 40s I tell myself...) and I am lost in the moment for an hour. It recharges my wellbeing batteries on every level. I highly recommend it.

Zumba has also become a vehicle for me to express my sexuality, simply by moving my body. Our culture constantly dictates to us that we need to look a certain way in order to be found attractive or sexy. Not enough emphasis is given to the fact that we are sexy *just the way we are.* So many people have the viewpoint that sexuality is to do with sexual preferences or the sexual act itself, but this is way off the mark. Our sexuality is a fundamental aspect of our identity. It's about quality of expression, not quantity of partners or how much sex we have. If you are interested, read Cabby Laffy who writes beautifully on the subject in her book *LoveSex.* Our sexuality is expressed in the clothes we wear, the jewellery we choose, the way we style our hair, the way we nurture our loved ones. How do you express your sexuality? Sadly, survivors of abuse are often completely disconnected to their bodies. This is a defensive response to the body that they feel betrayed them somehow and they carry shame. Shame is like a poison to the soul. It is always at the root of low self-worth. I managed to reconnect with my body, although it took a long time and happened gradually. My poetry helped me to capture this gentle process.

Difficult times of sadness, pain, stress, depression and anxiety come to us all. It's how we deal with them that makes the difference. Most people, myself included, try and fight the feelings that come, because of course they are not nice. But one of the most helpful things I have learned over my years of therapeutic work and training is to stop fighting it and *allow myself to feel,* even if it is painful. One of the first 'therapy-type' books I ever read was by Scott M Peck who wrote *The Road Less Travelled.* An old book now in therapeutic terms, but probably as relevant today as it ever was. One of the learnings from his book for me was to trust the wisdom of the unconscious that knows when an ending is needed; it's time to move on. Whether that be through the end of an unsatisfying relationship, a job that doesn't fulfil you anymore, a new home or something you've just outgrown and need to move beyond in order to continue to grow. Giving something up can feel like the pain of death, but when something dies or ends, it creates space and an opportunity for the birth of the new.

In my late 20s, I was left feeling bereft after a broken engagement. The life and future I had planned and looked forward to was dead to me. Instead of grieving, I suppressed all the painful feelings and spiralled downwards. I behaved badly for a while, didn't care about myself. That time created in me a lot of shame about some of the things I did, people I hurt and, most importantly, how I disrespected myself. Self-harm is the opposite to self-care. It doesn't have to mean physically hurting yourself, many of us self-harm without realising it. We drink too much, eat badly, gamble, pretend we're ok when we're not, abuse substances and other people, give ourselves away sexually too freely. At times like this, we attract others who are in the same place in their lives. I did. I had a number of harmful relationships at this time, you could say it opened up the old wound of sexual abuse which had lain dormant for so many years. I didn't feel worthy of being treated well, so that's what I got. I dishonoured my body and hated myself as a result.

This period ended with me becoming so ill, I nearly died. I developed Quinsy, a severe form of tonsillitis, which is rare now due to the use of antibiotics. However, it took me too long to look after myself, so I ended up in hospital. I had a golf-ball size abscess in my throat which made it increasingly difficult to breathe and swallow. It was very scary. I was plugged into a saline and antibiotic drip overnight and awoke the next morning to a sore but clear throat. I was told the severe pain I had experienced the day before (it was literally like someone drilling my ear) was the abscess bursting. Disgusting I know, but thankfully, I came through it. What followed was several weeks of massive amounts of pain killers and antibiotics and some serious R&R. I began to realise that my body was telling me to sit up and take notice. I couldn't continue treating myself this way. My time out provided me with a space for reflection – time for that 'third person' to consider where I was going with my life. I allowed myself to be sad. In fact, I was heartbroken, a most painful, terrible place to be. My defences had been built so high and wide, that no-one could get through. My heart was closed, and I was hurting inside. I told myself I would never get married and never have children. The fear of the pain of loss was so great. It may be a cliché, but time really does help recovery following loss because, as you move further away from the event, the intensity of the feelings lessen. But you never forget. Loss isn't just about death, it is experienced when anything comes to an end – relationships, jobs, a belief or idea about oneself, a chapter in life, moving house, the different stages of children growing up. It's all around us, always. No more so, than in the constant cycle of nature and the seasons. In winter, many things die off or go into hibernation, only to be reborn and blossom in the springtime. Human beings are biological cells, we are intrinsically linked to our natural environment, so we too experience continuous endings and beginnings. If we can learn to accept this as part of life, instead of fighting against it (a battle we can never win), we will find peace and grace within ourselves.

I meet people in the therapy room time and time again, who have had experiences or crisis-points in their lives which have forced them to stop. Depression and anxiety often mean people must stop working, even if for a short while, which allows them space to reflect. I now say to them, take this time and embrace it. Be curious about what your unconscious is trying to tell you. It's your friend and wants to help. Listen to your dreams; they are sent to help you understand your experience. Dreams, like creativity, provide a direct route into the

11

subconscious – which is where all the answers we need lie, waiting to be accessed.

In the end, as my body recovered, and I gained strength, I quit my job of 10 years which had been unsatisfying for some time, got a temporary evening job to enable me to finish my studies during the day and to help me keep paying the mortgage. I felt liberated. I was finally beginning to create my life as I wanted it to be. I very quickly felt better about all aspects of my life; I began to have a healthy relationship with myself, eating well, not drinking, exercising, discovering what I enjoyed doing. I got a bicycle and started going on long rides by myself, something I had loved doing as a child. I practiced yoga and meditation. I bought my own flat and lived on my own for the first time ever (I recommend this to everyone at least once in life!). It taught me so much about how capable, resilient, resourceful and strong emotionally I could be. Three months later, when I really wasn't looking, I met the man I was destined to marry. Fortunately, by then, I had learned that I deserved him, and I deserved to be happy and loved for me. Thirteen years later, not a day has gone by when I have doubted our relationship. I listened to the wisdom within and had the courage to follow my heart.

Becoming a mother was hard for me. My daughter was born nine weeks premature and there were huge amounts of stress and worry about her wellbeing. She hasn't had the easiest life, later developing Type 1 Diabetes aged five years, but her bravery and strength never ceases to amaze me. She is a prime example of how suffering can be transformed into extraordinary resilience. By the way, she is an incredibly talented artist and complete book worm. These two things help sustain her wellbeing. My son, now aged 9, is a warm, funny, friendly, caring, loving and kind child whose smile lights me up. I am incredibly proud of both of them and allow myself to take some of the credit for how they've turned out!

You will find in my poetry, artwork and photography, a lot of metaphor, meaning and symbolism. Once you access your creativity, this begins to flow towards you and you notice it all around you. I love photography and often capture an image that has spoken to me in some way. I was introduced to the idea of symbolism and its connection with the subconscious through the work of Carl Jung. In 2016, I undertook training in *Creative Arts Therapy*. I learned that everything has meaning. Colours, objects, images, words of course. But creative arts therapy is different to 'Art Therapy', where work is interpreted as a means of 'explanation'. Creative arts therapy has the person creating the work at its centre and therefore, the meaning that they give to it, is ultimately what makes it *meaningful*.

I'll give you an example. During this course, we were given a piece of clay and asked to represent ourselves at a certain point in our childhood. Usually when you do this kind of work, there is a moment where your mind goes completely blank and you have no idea what to do or what's about to happen. But herein lies the almost magical quality of working with the creative arts. You let go of any logical notion of what you want to create – you switch off your left brain (the analytical, thinking part) and switch on the right brain (the creative centre of feelings). The psyche stirs in those vital minutes. Slowly, my hands took the clay and I felt its cool, smooth, heavy weight. I gently squeezed and handled it for a while until my hands started to move, gently smoothing and caressing the clay. I allowed myself to just go with it. I created me, aged 9 years old, (this was my age when I was sexually abused by an old man in the village where I grew up). I made a model of myself, with very big feet. I believe this was to represent how I had to stand on my own two feet as a child, so they needed to be strong and large to carry and support me. I felt a huge amount of sadness and tenderness as I created myself, stroking the clay lovingly as I shaped that vulnerable little girl. My emotions were stirring. With another piece of clay, I began trying to make a cloak or blanket to cover me with, so I did my best to make it flat. I tried to place it over the model of me, but became really frustrated when it wouldn't stay put, it kept falling away. Eventually I managed to fix it in place, but felt it was unsatisfactory. It was only when I stood back and looked closely, that I saw something very different to my intention. I had been trying to create me, aged 9, with a cloak covering me. I was hiding under it for protection because this is how it felt for me back then. Being invisible, hidden and silent was safe. To be seen and heard meant danger; it was too risky. I could be exposed and abused again. I have learnt that many children who have been abused feel this way. But what I now saw was a child, not holding weakly onto the blanket to hide, but a strong figure, standing firm, pushing back the cloak behind me. I had an awareness that something significant had just happened, but it wasn't until sometime later, that I realised that this was the moment I moved from feeling like a victim, to seeing myself as a survivor. All because of a little bit of clay. This was a turning point for me.

Things began to move quickly for me then. Not long afterwards, I watched a Louis Theroux documentary about Jimmy Saville and witnessed the incredible bravery of some of the survivors, who'd had the most dreadful experiences of abuse. I couldn't get it out of my head, how strong they were to speak out, to be filmed speaking out and to be watched on national television. I was in awe of them. Something in me unleashed and I rang the police. I reported a crime that had been committed over thirty years ago. I had to go in and give a statement and I was given a crime number. It was now official. My husband held my hand the whole time. I can't tell you how cathartic it was. I had it confirmed that my abuser was dead, something I knew intuitively anyway, but it was a relief that I could draw a line under it. I walked out of that police station shaking like a leaf, but with my head high and shoulders back. That part of my story was finished, and I wanted to move forward with my life. In March 2017, I published *Mending the Soul. A Journey Beyond Abuse.* I think, with hindsight, it was my way of saying that I refuse to be silent and invisible anymore. I want to be known for all I am.

Another theme throughout my poetry is nourishment and healing. Again, Carl Jung has been hugely influential to me through his ideas connecting the difficulties, trauma and suffering of life with the concept of emotional and psychological wounding. We all have our scars, some are deeper than others. Jung developed the idea of the psyche being divided into two parts. The persona contains the parts of ourselves that we show to the world; the part we are accepting of, we don't mind others seeing. The other part is the shadow, the part of our psyche that we do not accept. So, we try to keep it covered up, due to shame, fear or embarrassment and defences such as avoidance or denial. When I created my clay figure; went to the police and published my book, this was my way of casting off my shadow. When we deny the shadow, we feed its power to impinge on our lives by allowing the soul to remain fragmented. When we develop the courage to face our fears, we are liberated and can reconnect those shattered pieces. We can create a new way of

13

being.

Jung believed that the function and purpose of the psyche is to move towards a return to its original state – whole and pure. Just as it is when we are born. The trials of life result in the psyche becoming distorted and fragmented, until in adulthood (often mid-life), we reach a point of crisis about who we truly are. We have developed our identity according to the external messages of our parents, peers, society etc and we have moved further and further away from our authentic Self. Layer upon layer is constructed. This is why children are so much more in touch with their creativity and imaginations; they have fewer layers because they are younger. As adults, our subconscious tries to speak to us, tries to tell us that something is wrong. Depression and anxiety are often manifestations of this. The question is, do we listen? Or have we become so disconnected to our inner-world, so attached to the mask that we wear to disguise our true identity, that we can't hear the messages at all? So, we try all sorts of things to feel better. One of them is coming to therapy with the idea that a therapist will 'fix us'. He or she will have all the answers, will patch us up and send us on our way. We can get back to work, carry on in our unhappy (but safe) lives without upsetting the applecart. It couldn't be further from the truth. People in therapy (if they have a good therapist) very quickly learn that's not how it works. They must take responsibility for their own lives which requires self-discipline and developing a more flexible mind-set. They must learn that self-harming is destroying their soul and they need to develop more self-compassion.

I am trained in CBT (Cognitive Behavioural Therapy) and believe it has its place in helping people develop more positive ways of thinking. But it falls short of 'treating' the whole person. If a crisis is experienced within the soul, learning to manage your thinking will only take you so far. What's also needed is balance and healing in the other three areas of wellbeing – your physical, emotional and spiritual wellbeing. If you are very self-critical or judgemental or you tend to catastrophise (always look at the 'worst case scenario'), it's important to understand what is underneath this way of being. Understanding and growing self-awareness make self-compassion more possible. Instead of living in the fear of, for example, being terrible at your job; ask yourself, what is it that I need to do in order to be better? Or, what is it that might be holding me back? Or, focus on what you do well to find a balance. In this way of considering and questioning yourself, self-compassion begins to grow.

You may notice in my poetry references to the process of alchemy, an ancient process where ordinary matter is transformed into gold. This is another Jungian concept used as symbolism for the human capacity to transform difficult, painful experiences into positive, meaningful ones; from darkness into light. In couples therapy, I see the relationship as a container into which each partner has the capacity to pour in both their good and bad aspects and have them transformed into gold. Our partner holds up a mirror to our authenticity (or lack of it) and sometimes we don't like what we see. Relationships are a minefield of projections and it takes great courage to ask the question, what am I expecting of my partner that I ought to be doing for myself? For example, I never considered myself to be adventurous, I had not particularly travelled or taken many risks. So, what did I do? I married a man who was a sky-diver, scuba-diving instructor from a different part of the world who had travelled South America on his own for two years (nearly dying in dodgy exploits on a couple of occasions). Guess what I was unconsciously projecting onto him? That if I am with this man, he will *make me* more adventurous. So, in the early years, I looked to him to plan our adventures, I made him *responsible* for that role in our relationship. It wasn't until I realised that this was happening that I was able to take ownership of my responsibility to *share* this role, that our relationship changed. It's still not something that comes easily to me (old habits die hard), but I now know that I have the capacity to be adventurous. We all do, of course.

Creativity helps to assimilate and synthesize all aspects of the fragmented psyche and helps to promote balance in the four elements of wellbeing – physical, mental, emotional and spiritual. You could liken it to an orchestra playing in perfect unison, or a harmony of voices; a piece of art or movie or book that touches your soul. Your subconscious speaks to you, you hear it and it makes sense. Always be curious about moments in your life where your subconscious, or you could call it intuition too, is trying to tell you something. Robert Johnson, a Jungian who writes about relationships and balance advocates that symbolic meaning speaks to our subconscious not to tell us what we already know, but to show us what we have yet to learn. Creativity helps reconnect that which has become disconnected.

I encourage you to practice mindfulness every day. Being mindful is really just allowing yourself to be in the present moment, activating all your five senses. It doesn't mean you need to sit and meditate for hours on end. Notice and observe what's around you; the colour of the sky, the sound of children playing, the perfumes of the blossom, the taste of the coffee in your hand, the warmth of the sun on your skin. Drink it all in. Even in a traffic jam, instead of allowing the tension and frustration to mount; listen to music you like, look at the sky, let your mind wander to a happy memory, notice and observe. Breathe. The stress hormone, Cortisol, will be pumping through your system because you are stressed but as soon as you begin to relax, the brain will get the message that the 'threat' ("I'm going to be late") which is making you feel stressed, has passed. It will stop releasing the hormone. There is no greater cure for stress than breathing mindfully. Speak to the birds, animals and trees as you pass by. Acknowledge them, say hello. Embrace everything around you. Let the complete spectrum of life encircle you. Don't fear sadness or pain, have faith that it will not destroy you and you will develop new knowledge that will help you in the future when you face challenges. Nothing is a failure if you learn from it. Regret is futile and just creates negative energy. Making mistakes helps us to grow and be better. Don't let self-criticism eat away at your soul. Develop a flexible mindset when overcoming difficulties and obstacles. There is always another way. Occasionally we are met with a 'lighthouse', an immoveable object, person or event in our lives – something beyond our control. The secret then is to recognise it for what it is and then you have a choice. You can either bash yourself on the rocks trying to change it and damage and deplete yourself, or you can accept it and find a way around and beyond it. Let it go. Move on.

When a person begins to heal, they do so in different ways. When I speak of *nourishment*, I am not just talking about food. Although, what we put into our bodies, is hugely reflective of how we feel about them. Do we treat them kindly or abuse them? Our bodies do the most incredible job, we need to honour and respect them and give them what they need to flourish. If you put cheap fuel in your car, you will likely do it some damage. Same thing for our bodies. So, the physical aspect of wellbeing, requires us to eat and drink mindfully. To forgo things that damage us like smoking or drinking alcohol excessively. It sends a message, 'I am taking care of myself', which ultimately translates into "I love myself". This requires self-discipline which is not always easy. Old habits die hard they say, but Neuroscience, the study of the brain, now tells us that the brain is plastic, not solid and rigid as was once believed, so it is pliable and can change. This is such positive news for anyone who wants to develop new ways of doing things. Neural pathways are created in the brain every time we learn or develop a new skill or idea, like learning to drive or speak a foreign language etc. It takes around six months for a neural pathway to fully develop and, around the same time for an old unused pathway to die off. So, if we make a promise to ourselves that we will cut down on the amount of alcohol we drink, we need to commit to this timescale to really make a difference. Sometimes, it doesn't take that long, depending on what it is we're trying to change. This news is extremely hopeful as it confirms, scientifically, the possibility for change.

Nourishment of the *soul*, for me, comes from being with nature, dancing or singing, watching a meaningful movie or reading a great book, being with my children, spending time with my husband or a good friend, looking at art, being creative (gardening, home decorating and designing, cooking, writing). What nourishes you and makes you feel good about yourself? Take some time to consider this. Equally, think about what or who do you find toxic in your life? And can you do anything about this? It's helpful to consider what you do to take care of yourself and make changes if necessary.

Roberto Assagioli, the father of the Psychosynthesis movement, talks of the 'awakening experience'. These are times of enlightenment and growing self-understanding. I call them 'lightbulb moments'. You know, that moment where you say, 'Oh yeah!', the penny has dropped, something in your subconscious that you always knew, has risen to the surface and is being fully acknowledged. Not surprisingly, it happens a lot to people in therapy. Assagioli says that often, what follows an awakening experience, is a desire to cleanse and purify. This may come in the form of physically taking better care of yourself, perhaps re-evaluating relationships, your work, your environment, your hopes and beliefs. He speaks of it at the deepest level, as a purification of the soul. There is a parallel here with Jung's ideas about returning to a pure soul state. A clearing out of the clutter accumulated through life, an urge to simplify. When we do this, we create space for a new way of being. Where there once may have been negativity, anxiety and fear, we can now experience feeling more in control of our lives, *creating* our lives as we want them to be. Alongside this comes the increased capacity to feel wonder, awe and joy. We have space for it. This capacity balances with the sadness and pain we may have had to come through in order to get to a certain point in our lives. In fact, Assagioli even goes as far as to say that suffering has a direct impact on helping the soul to become free. It's a pre-requisite. An awakening experience can bring about a lightness of the spirit, a feeling of expansion; a new sense of inner-security and power. Harmony in the inner world.

If you met me, I believe you would experience me as a very warm, open-hearted, loving person. This is how I feel about myself. I have nothing to hide and I do not allow fear to hold me back. I believe I am authentic, what you see is what you get! Recently, I spent some time at a Quaker meeting house and was amazed by the environment. It was like being immersed in a warm bath of love, gentleness, kindness and acceptance. The people I met were open and friendly, it was a unique and unusual experience. I am not someone of a particular religious faith, but I do consider myself to be a very spiritual person. In my mind, our humanity connects us all, regardless of our faith, gender, sexual preference, nationality, culture etc. I believe that, deep down, we all want to live simply with the people we love, to treat others with respect and kindness and expect the same in return. I am an optimist and humanist at heart and feel the troubles of the wider world very deeply, it's an aspect of my 'highly intuitive and sensitive' nature. (If this resonates with you, look up Heidi Sawyer who writes beautifully on this subject).

I often have periods of not listening to the radio or watching the news because the enormity of the world's troubles can overwhelm me, and I end up feeling so helpless. No wonder so many people suffer with anxiety, the world is a scary place. I've learnt to recognise when I need to tune out for a little while and recommend people I am working with who suffer with depression and/or anxiety to do the same. It's all part of self-care. I try to be friendly and open. I wouldn't walk past another human being without saying hello or smiling. I don't understand a culture that sees people staring at a screen rather than engaging with a fellow human being. No wonder people feel so isolated and lonely. This is one of the reasons I limit my time in highly-populated places, like cities. After a few hours, I sense the disconnection of the people around me to such a degree that I begin to find it unbearable. It worries me what kind of world we are creating for our young people. I've come to the conclusion that all I can do, is look after others in the ways I know how to, by being a good wife, mother, daughter, sister, friend and therapist. These are the things that bring meaning to my life.

I am most happy amongst nature and the theme of the natural world is prominent in my poetry. One of my favourite things to do, is walk my dog in the woods near to where we live. I feel completely at peace there and, recently, feel very connected to my late mum in those moments. The natural world is full of beauty but flawed, it reminds us that this is also the case for the human condition. Nature tells us that nothing ever stays the same, nothing is permanent or forever. And when we are in a dark place, that can be a huge comfort.

I appreciate that I am probably too intense for some people. But that's ok. That belongs to them. What I mean by that, is that it's important that we all take responsibility for our own boundaries. I often work with people struggling with issues around boundaries in relationships. If in our early years, we didn't have good boundaries or the opposite, if the boundaries were too rigid or strict, we can struggle as adults to know where to draw the line. And, essentially, that is what's required. To draw a line between you and another person. To learn that you are responsible for your 50% and the other person is responsible for their 50%. We've all come across people in life who try to encroach on our 50% - we experience them as dominant, oppressive, suffocating, bossy, controlling, abusive. And generally, they are not really interested in our 50%. They are, at heart, afraid.

They feel they need to dominate and control in order to feel safe. They will have been made this way through their personal experiences of relationships. If we *allow* them to treat us this way, it's important to recognise that we are colluding with them. It's not fair to blame them, we need to fight for our 50%, even if it causes conflict. On the flip side, some people will do everything in their power to *not* take responsibility. They allow *you* to encroach on their 50% (even if you don't want to), because again, they are afraid. They would rather let you take responsibility either because they feel inadequate or because they are lazy. The balance of 'power' in relationships is key and always rears its head when working with couples. It manifests in two main areas -sex and money. Where there is power and control, there is no equality, and this breeds resentment and competitiveness, instead of support and encouragement. Communication breaks down, anger develops, and empathy evaporates. In couples therapy, working on inner balance as individuals, provides the platform to develop a new way of communicating in relationships. Empathy then becomes possible, communication flourishes as one becomes fully emotionally available.

Mine has been very much an inner journey. You may have had a different experience. Perhaps you have travelled the world and done lots of adventurous things, but inside, you feel there is work to do. As I write this, I am spending a few days by the Norfolk coast. I recognised that in order to write, I needed space and freedom to just be. Isaac Newton had his famous 'aha!' moment of insight, discovering gravity, whilst sitting under a tree relaxing. Our greatest insights come when we allow ourselves to be in the moment and our brain is resting. This is when the subconscious can be accessed and it has all the answers we seek. Creativity then flows.

I have realised, as I write, that this book is about much more than my poetry, it is ultimately my story. Therapy provides a space to tell your story, the narrative of your life. It takes courage and I do feel brave opening myself up to you like this. But being heard, understood and acknowledged by another human being is a basic human need and is what brings people to the therapy room time after time. It follows a particularly difficult time in my life, having lost my mum to cancer a few months earlier. She had been battling it for eighteen months and put up a good fight, but it got her in the end. Never in my life have I been more aware of the power of endings to transform into new beginnings. I allow myself to feel the sadness of my loss, but at the same time, I am able to see that this is a new chapter in my life, one without my mum. It has created space for a new relationship with my dad, a most welcome outcome that brings me great joy.

Most psychologists agree that the relationship between mother and child is *the* most important relationship of all, the template from which all other relationships in our lives stem. As I experienced an inner-transformation in recent years, I also noticed my relationship with my mum transform. I moved to a position of being able to understand, empathise and forgive things that had happened in my past. I owned my projections and took responsibility for my part in things. This allowed me to stop blaming and, ultimately, open up my heart to my mum – and my dad - in a new way. Thank goodness I did, because sadly, we didn't have a lot of time left. The last words we said to one another were of our love for one another and the last memory I have is of her gentle touch. This gives me great comfort and peace.

In western culture, we are 'time-poor', we have busy, full lives. There is guilt attached to doing something simply for ourselves. The word 'selfish' is seen as a negative. But, actually, addressing the needs-of-the-self is essential for a rewarding life and to find peace within. The greatest gift we can give ourselves is time. Time to gather our thoughts and feelings; time to be with the ones we love and give them our full attention; time to acknowledge, address and honour our needs. Give yourself permission to take some time for yourself. Develop good boundaries. Switch off your mobile phone and clock off from work at a decent time. No-one else can do it for you. It is your responsibility. Find your voice and use it. Say what you need to say and be heard. Tell your story, it's so cathartic. Be authentic, let go of the mask and the shadow. Ask for what you want and need. People are not mind-readers. Be assertive. Be brave. And you will live a rich and worthy life.

Motherhood

Shopping Trip

Seatbelts on, engine starts
Ready to go

Swaying to the music
Laughing and clapping

Nathan says "mama...bus!"
And my heart melts like warm fudge sauce

Park the car
Find a trolley – bums on seats
Ready to go

Push, push, around the aisles
Grab this, grab that
Can't hang about

They're laughing and smiling but
Any minute now
There'll be hair pulling and crying

Throw things in
That'll do

Phew!
Made it with no to-do

Kids eh, who'd have them?

Squabbling, fighting, vying for my attention
Me, piggy in the middle
Referee extraordinaire

Oh, but how wonderful they are
What a miracle of nature
Perfectly formed
Beauty personified
Innocent
Curious
Bursting with love

That moment when they take your hand
Walking through the snow
So tiny and warm
Enclosed in your protective clasp

Kids eh? Who'd have them?
Me, me, me
Every time

What about Me?

Mummy mummy mummy...
Demand after demand
Coming think and fast
The needs of young children...endless
Doorbell chimes
Telephone rings
And what about hubby?
He doesn't get a look in

And what about me?
Ok...deep breath....

Answer door, answer telephone
Tidy, clean, iron, cook, play....

Is it bedtime yet?!

Cup of tea in my hand
Comfy sofa
All is quiet and peaceful
Am I done?

But hang on a minute
We had fun, didn't we?
And I survived!

I'm pretty awesome really you know
I managed it all
Resilient, strong, practical
And loving
The most important thing of all

Full of Love

I am full of love
It's bursting from within me
Seeping through my pores

Enveloping all I meet

In my mind
I picture my children
Smiling, giggling, playing

And my heart overflows with love.

Honest Mummy

Oh, what bliss
The stillness and peace
Of a quiet house

Children at school
A time to reflect

Yes, the chores need doing

But just let me breathe……

Cycling home
I see the convoy of mummies
With pushchairs and toddlers in toe

A frenzy of scooters and activity

Frazzled mums trying desperately to control their offspring
Lonely mums trying desperately to connect

Later, at the school gates
The mums converge
For 5 minutes, twice a day

They make semblance of friendship
Or is it more camaraderie?

Is there a difference?

Any closeness I may have felt to these whirling dervishes
Is purely an illusion

One, I know I have created

But, let's be honest
No friendship is to be found here

My Precious Girl

I cannot begin to describe
How much I love you
My precious girl

You have brought light and laughter into my life
A golden glow of warmth and joy

Your battles have been many
Even at this tender age

But the strength you show
Is something to behold

I wish I could protect you from the ills of this world
I wish I could take away your faulty body
And bring you a shiny, new one
Wrapped in a silver bow

So that you may feel the freedom and innocence
That is a child's right

But as I can't do that
I will be here, always
Holding your little hand
And keeping you close to my heart

Mummy is here
My precious girl
Forever and always

Here for You

You are my purpose in life
You are the reason my heart beats
Why my eyes smile
You are my world
My universe

Two little souls
With joy in your hearts
Giggles and mischief on your minds!

Your innocence cleanses me
Your simplicity uncomplicates me

The touch of your tiny hands in mine
Is heavenly

I am here for you my precious angels
Forever and always
Whenever
And however
You need me to be

I will protect you
And keep you safe
Help you grow and learn
I will be a shoulder to lean on
And an ever-ready hug

My children
My life

Harmony

Every moment is precious
Making love
Only breathing
Talking with loved ones
Images in the clouds
Opening my heart
Nathan's hand in mine
April's giggly tickles
Love everywhere

Sounds of birdsong
Pounding of my heart
Imagining
Remembering
Intensity of the moment
Time stands still
Universe brings me gifts
All is calm inside
Love everywhere

Mother earth
Enough – for me
Nurturing
Trampolining fun
Allowing myself to let go
Love everywhere

Playing
Hooray for holidays
Yesterday is history
Sounds of the trees
Inspired
Cuddling until your heart could burst
Attunement
Love – for all

Conflict

Liberation comes at a cost.

I am caught between
A desire to achieve and succeed
And a longing, aching desire
To just be here for you
I tell myself, "there will be time for me"
But is this true?
How much time do I have left?
My potential has been waiting patiently
But now, it seems.
It calls to me
With more urgency

Technology

Wired up
Lugged in
Switched on

No escape
Always available
Calibrated and
Tuned in

I just want to be free from it
To unplug and tune out

My poor little girl
Attached to machines
Every second of her life

I hope the day will come
When she can be free of all this

What Is Love?

When you love someone
With all your heart
Unconditionally
Their heart, happiness, fulfilment
Become treasures to admire, nurture and care for

Sometimes you may need to
Sacrifice your own fulfilment
To provide a space, light and water
For theirs to grow

But if you can do this
With a gentle smile
A benevolent heart
And the knowledge that
This is the right thing for the one you love

Then your reward
Will be great
For when you need fulfilment
They will return the favour
And nourish you right back

The Natural World

The Chill

Chilly to the bone
Jack Frost has visited today
Sprinkles of glitter
Shimmer in the sun

The weeping willow
Bends gracefully to the ground
It's fingers skimming the hard earth
Tickling it softly

The trees are majestic
Coated in glittering paint
The fields brushed by an artist
In a monochrome style

The spiders' webs in every nook and cranny
Visible now, sparkling white
Looping the loop along the fences
Dancing their way along

Looking into the distance
My heart soars at the sheer beauty
Of this wondrous day

Snow

The world is a beautiful place today
The snow covers all
Like someone poured thick cream
Over the contours of the land

On the bridge
It seems one hundred fairies have thrown
One hundred tiny snowballs
Splattering onto the bricks

The trees stretch out their limbs
Desperate to be covered
In the silky cream

Like excitable children vying for attention
"Me next!" "No, me first!"

Even the rubbish bin looks majestic
With a luxurious white robe
Draped over its noble shoulders

All is clean and pure
A new beginning
A fresh start
New eyes
To view the world

It's not the snow that's magical
I feel it from within

Strength

I'm as strong as an Oak
That's observed this world for centuries
Entwined with the earth and matter
Yet standing independently above

The winds and seasons
Move and sway my branches
But my trunk remains firm

I know who I am
I know I am a survivor
People have tried to cut me down
But I remain strong

All those lessons learned
All that wisdom absorbed

I feel like the luckiest Oak alive
Privileged
Enlightened
Liberated

Playing

The lime green leaves
Wink cheekily at me in the sun

The branches reach across the path
To tickle one another
Right before my eyes

The brown leaves on the ground
Dance and bounce along in the wind
Like excited toddlers

All this fun and playfulness
It's all around us
If we know *how* to look

Space to Breathe

The whispering wind in the trees
The warmth of the sun on my skin
The distant sounds of children playing
The clouds sliding silently across the blue expanse above me

The words of wisdom and enlightenment
At my fingertips
The ancient messages and truths
Soaking into my being
Dissolving into my soul
Healing my wounds
Creating space and possibilities
For a new outlook

I inhale and breathe in the space around me
No demands, no expectations
Just me, my body and the benevolence of nature around me
Cleansing and renewing every fibre of my being

The past is behind me
The future unknown
Now is what matters

Self-compassion

My Inner-child

I see her in my Winnie-the-Poo mug
In the snowy penguin paper-weight
I see her now in the mirror
My inner child....

Hello my friend
Where have you been?
Locked away for so long
In a cold and lonely place
Silent
Invisible
Waiting to be discovered

It's so good to meet you
At last

The past cannot hurt you now
It's safe
To come out and play

Hello my friend
Stay a while
The world is waiting for you

Me

Is that really me?
The mirror doesn't lie, they say

But look at my hair
It's so shiny and soft
And my skin is silky and smooth

Could my eyes really be that blue?

Should I be saying this?
Perhaps I'm being vain

But look again….

Now, I see clearly
It *is* me that I see
Me from the inside
And I am beautiful

I Love Myself

It started with my reflection
I see my kind face and eyes
I look deeper
And see
A benevolent heart
A huge capacity to heal
My smile reaches my eyes
And brings comfort and peace
To others

Then I saw it in my actions
Allowing time and space for myself
A luxury for a working wife and mother
A cycle ride
Just to feel the wind in my hair
A coffee and a cake
Just because I can

Finally, I felt it in my body
The softness of my skin
The shine in my hair
The pale blue of my eyes
The warmth from within
Healing, nurturing and caring
For me

Learning self-compassion, self-love
Helped repair the wounds of the past
Helped restore the connection
Between body, mind and soul

Now I'm able to focus my attention forwards
Instead of being stuck in the past
To enjoy the moment
To delight in pleasure

To start anew.

Quiet

Please turn off the light
It hurts my eyes
All they want to do is rest

Wrap me up in a warm, soft blanket
Let me stretch out my aching limbs
My head craves stillness
My body, the same

Turn off the phones and computers
Surely, I won't be missed for a little while
The world is a scary place sometimes
And I need to withdraw

Snuggle into my nest
And remember to breathe again
Zone out
Switch off
Recharge my depleted batteries

So that I can bounce back again
Renewed and energised
For whatever life offers up next....

Substance

Weighty, rounded and full
Plush, ripe and velvety
Contours that curve
Rhythm in movement

My body feels voluptuous
Womanly. Sexy
Hourglass

I feel more substantial
Not frail like a twig
About to snap at any moment

The strength comes from within
The roots grow deeper and further
Into the solid, nurturing earth

I delight in it
I allow it to wash over me
The glowing light of self-compassion

Tired

I'm so tired
The world seems to be turning more slowly
No energy to do the things I want to do
Just enough
To get me through the days

But what about fun and laughter?
Pleasure and excitement?
Motivation and drive?

They are snuggled up
Inside me somewhere
Snoozing quietly

Everything is an effort
I give too much of my energy
To my children
To my clients
There's not enough left
For me
Or my love

I'm sluggish
Slow
Wading through treacle
I'm bent and crooked
Tense and tight
Aches and pains all over

No more

I need some TLC
I need to awaken my vitality
My 'Joie de Vivre'

But for now
I'll be kind and loving towards myself
Rest
Be still and calm
And heal.

Self-compassion

I feel the warm glow of the sun on my skin
And it blends with the warmth I feel inside
The old wounds have been opened again
And I have been suffering

Small, vulnerable and quiet
But the difference now is that instead of shame
I feel so much love – for me

Where once there lived inside me
A spiky, hard mine
Ready to explode on impact
Of self-criticism and pain

Now there exists a warmth
A softness within

It wasn't my fault
I grieve what I have lost
Innocence and the ignorance of such emotional pain

But I am stronger than ever
And the wound heals a little more

And so, my journey continues….

Cathy

How can I ever thank you?
For the precious gift
You bestowed on me

You showed me how to
Open my heart
And let love flow freely

Without your guidance
I may never have known
That I was holding on

It was a moment on my journey
That I will never forget

Opening the door to my heart
Led to letting go

My creativity has set me free

And through this
I developed the greatest gift of all

I learned how to love myself

Love Light

Let the warm glow of love
Bathe you in its magnificence

Lift up your eyes and your soul
Open up your heart and your arms
Embrace all that you deserve

To be adored
To be admired
To be cherished

Cast aside the shadows of the past
Nurture your bruised heart
Nourish your soul

For you are deeply loveable
Allow yourself to feel it

Always Remember

Always remember
You are allowed to feel sad
And it's ok to let others see
Your sorrow
Your vulnerability

Always remember
You are allowed to feel angry
It channels your strength and passion
You make yourself heard
You cannot be ignored

Always remember
You are allowed to feel unwell
At times when your resources are low
Treat yourself kindly
With compassion and love

Always remember
You are allowed to be quiet
Words don't always provide you with what you need
Noise can be a distraction
From your inner wisdom

Always remember
You are allowed to ask for what you need
When you require extra strength or comfort
You can open up your arms
And be acknowledged by another

The Awakening Self

Potential

I'm 10ft tall
I'm walking on air
Liberated
Invigorated

I'm good at this
But I always knew, didn't I?
Oh, but what wonderful validation.

The sky's the limit
I can do anything

Nothing like pushing beyond
Your comfort zone.
To grow and renew

Well done me.

Empty House

There was a time
When empty meant lonely

Lost
Drifting

Now the bliss of a quiet house
The ticking of the clock
The birdsong outside

It's like the warm surrender
Of a tired body
As it drifts away from the thinking world
And enters the place of rest and dreams

No place to be
No-one needs me

Ecstasy

40

What a momentous milestone
A pinpoint in time
I feel liberated from concerns
Of my younger days
Exhilarated by the prospect
Of 40 more years to come

Limitless learning and growing
Like the ancient oak tree
That gathers strength
Increasing its roots
Year upon year

I see the number
I see how my body has changed
I see the wrinkles and scars
The signs of life
And time passing

But if my skin was like a suit
That I'm meant to grow into
Each year that passes
It fits me more and more

I've learnt to love this physical body
And treat it with respect and compassion
It houses my inner-being
It provides a vehicle to express myself
It speaks to me when all is not well….

And I need to take notice…

Transience

I see a woman
Looking into the horizon
Her gaze is serene and tranquil

She looks beyond
What others see
She feels entwined with the rising sun

Her hair lifts and falls gently on the breeze
The dark, soft strands stretch out behind her
The blue of her eyes reflects the sky

Her physical body is strong and lean
The confidence of self-knowledge
Glows from within her

She consumes this moment
As if it were her last
And as I watch her from afar
The knowledge of who she is
Trickles warmly through my body

She is part of me
The me, I aspire to be

In the Sand

Like Creatures from the Deep
Having lain quiet and still
They rise to the surface
In a crashing wave of affect

The echoes of the past
Vibrate and resonate
Like the notes played skillfully
On an instrument of strings

I open up my heart to let it flow
I trust that tranquil waters will return
Once the tsunami
Has passed through

But there is no devastation
To clear up afterwards
Only a rainbow to show
That pot of valuable treasure

For anyone who has experienced
The stirring of the psyche
The letting go of hurt and pain
Within the grains of sand
Knows the precious truth

In order to heal
We must first open the wound
But once vulnerable
We release our formidable power
To repair

Coming Out

It's not what you think
I'm not gay!
But I have been hiding

And I don't want to anymore

Just like the baby in peek-a-boo
I want to be seen
Really seen

Because *I* have been looking closely
And I like what I see
I *love* what I see

The beauty of my soul takes my breathe away

So maybe if I show you myself
You will love me too?
All of me

Can you look beyond the scars?
Can you see the strength behind the vulnerability?

We are all many things
Far from simple

My journey has brought me to this point
Where I am able to transcend the pain and suffering
Of that wonderful, innocent little girl

So, if I come out to play
Will you play with me?

Three Doves

As I watch
Filled with peace and calm
The three doves
Take flight

They look so beautiful
Liberated, free

As they sore high in the blue sky
My heart lifts up towards the heavens

They are taking with them
My pain
My sadness
My loss

I smile as I watch them go
Their leaving enables me to be free

I am left with a heart
That feels light
And pure
And golden

Ready to create
Free to fully love
Alive
Awake
Healed

Lava Lamp

Picture a lava lamp
At first glance
Its contents seem still and tranquil
Sleeping

Then, the first bubble
Begins to take shape
You watch it closely
As it forms, breaks free
And slowly rises to the surface

This is how it feels for me
The pain, the sadness
The loss of innocence
It lays sleeping, undisturbed
Mostly

Then, a little bubble of memory
or emotion
Is triggered
And it begins its ascent
It gently reaches the surface
And I remember
And I feel it again

Sometimes the bubble is huge
it grows and expands
Then releases its grip on the base
Making its way upwards

It explodes on the surface
A tsunami of emotion
My whole body shakes
The tears pour out of me
Like an uncontrollable torrent

And then....

Like the beach after the storm
There is a stillness like no other
The ghost has been exorcised
The demon unleashed
The fever is fading

I am healed a little more
The waters are calm again once more

Messenger

I know you've come to tell me
That time is running out
Since the moment I awoke
You have remained like a stuck record
In my head

That moment of annihilation
(Or so I thought)
Brought me to this realisation

The blinding light
Will lead my way

I need to make changes
I need to focus
I need to be fulfilled
I need to feel whole

Growing Balls

I'm not afraid anymore
To say what I think
To trust what I feel
To ask for what I need

I've 'manned up'
I've found my inner masculinity
A balance for the nurturing soul
I have truly become

I notice my growing confidence
I observe a deep inner calm
I smile as I feel the sashaying
Of my hips as I walk!

I am my own woman
I know who I am
Head high, shoulders back
Striding with purpose towards the horizon

The Awakening

It's time to wake up
And wipe the blurred sleep of denial
From your eyes

And really see

You can take off the mask
No need to pretend anymore
Stop looking outside yourself
For love, acknowledgement, reassurance and praise
And instead, look inward

The make-up that disguises you
The clothes that hide you
The career that defines you
The relationship you believe you can't survive without

You don't need any of them
They are not who you are

So, face your fear
Wake up to your mortality
Grab this precious life by the horns
And liberate yourself

Come out and be seen
Embrace who you are
Don't be afraid to look into your shadows
For there, you will find wisdom
They will not destroy you

Look upward and marvel
At the awesomeness of nature
Feel the warmth of the sun on your skin
Allow yourself to hear the birdsong
Nurture and nourish yourself

To be fully awake
Is to be authentic
To be authentic
Is to be fully alive

Endings and Beginnings

K

Young love
First love

Forgive me
I'm so sorry
For hurting you…

Twice

I envied you
So comfortable with yourself
Connected to your soul

Not me
I was troubled
Not free

I never understood
What you heard in the music
What you saw in the sunset
Or the silhouette of my body

But now I do
Now I get it

I hope you are happy
And as uncomplicated
As you once were

I hope I have not scarred you

Always remember
That I loved you
Completely

Once

S

You hurt me
Why?
What did I ever do to you?

But love you
And care for you

You cheated and lied
Manipulated me

Did it feel good?
Make you feel powerful?
In control, in some way?

Because, of course, you never were

You were just a boy
I see it now

Lost and alone
Desperate for love
But fearing it

So, you pushed me away
Well done
You did me a favour

But as for you?
You're hurting still

Leaving Me

Abandoned
Betrayed
You're leaving me

I'm falling, falling
Where's the ground?

I've lost my footing
The rug has been pulled

You coward
No explanation

And then you're gone

So many questions

I trusted you completely
I was wrong

And now I'm trapped in a whirlwind
Freedom
Excitement
Independence

But it's not real
It's too fragile
And I am vulnerable
And scared underneath

So disconnected
From my core

The tears have dried
But the betrayal runs deep.

The Black Dog

We've met before
You and I

But you don't scare me anymore

Now I ask myself
"Why did you visit this time?"
"What is it that I need to learn?"

When you're around me
I feel your weight heavy on my shoulders

Your negative breath
Hot on my neck

And as you turn to leave
I feel the day begin to brighten

I can smile at people I meet
And open my heart to love and joy again

Each time
I feel renewed

A new chapter begins

Full of the knowledge
Of what you have taught me

I am strong
I am resilient
I am powerful
I am a good person
I am a loving mother, daughter, wife

I reconfirm my place in the world.

A Good Day

Today is going to be a good day

The tears and troubles of recent days
Are retreating into the shadows

I feel my strength returning
My head is high, and my step assured

The future is on the horizon

And the sun is coming up.

Narrow

Restricted
Limited
Trapped
Suffocated
Claustrophobic
Can't eat this
Can't do what you want
When you want
No time
No space
Overwhelming
Over stimulation
Can't grow
Must heal and repair
Depleted resources

Then….
The flower begins to blossom again
The petals gently unfurl
And face the sunshine
I can breathe
And think
And feel
I can grow
And learn
Be creative
Be free

Not the End

This is not the end
It's just the beginning

My new eyes are sparkly and bright
Ready to see the world anew

An alternate reality
A fresh perspective

Based on strength, courage
Determination and compassion

I feel the earth firmly beneath my feet
And yet wings raise me up

Beyond the everyday
To a new place
Of enlightenment and resolve

It's my time to shine.

Leaving

We're leaving now
Never to return
But we don't leave empty handed

You can't see it
Or touch it
But you have given us so much

Like the shiny stars above us
Your gifts are constant and eternal

You've given us your love
Your time
Your kindness
You've seen us learn and grow and learn

We have captured this in our hearts
And they are fuller and more open
For what they have received

So even though we are leaving
To embrace pastures new
We will take a little piece
Of all you have given us
And treasure it forever

Walking Towards the Sun

It begins with baby steps
Feeling the way gently and with trepidation
Overcome by powerful emotions
Falling, letting go, converging
With the soul of another

There proceeds a stillness in time
The world around fades in significance
All that matters is here and now
Two souls entwined, connected as one
Until the wounds of the past begin to open
And the magic sparkle slowly dies

Many times, my heart has ascended
Towards the dizzy heights of love
Intoxicated by the feelings
Lured by the promise of everlasting contentment
Each time my heart was captured
It opened up and was flooded with love
Only to slowly and sadly close
As the dream faded and reality descended

My heart may be a little battered and bruised
It may have felt the heights of ecstasy
And the depths of despair
But it restores and repairs itself, in time
And comes back fighting
Ready to love again

The journey of love is fraught with risk
And bliss
Each step of the way we can be blinded
By the intensity of the light
Or lost in the shadows of the darkness

Here, now, my heart has found peace
A lasting contentment
A sense of belonging
A balance between the burning of the sun
And the cold and dark of loneliness

My heart is warm and cherished by another

Was it all worth it?

Undoubtedly. Yes.

Indifference

It's as though you want us here
And yet you don't

Your arms are open and yet as we enter
You withdraw them

You want to be close to us
But you don't
Perhaps you don't know how to

Whatever I say to you doesn't feel right
I am uncertain around you

How can I break this well-worn path?
Or should I continue as before?

I want to understand you
For us to know one another better

I cannot see a way ahead
So, I will take each step
One at a time

Thorn

You have been there
For far too long

Each time I reached forwards
You tore at my skin
Restricting me
Holding me back

The day I ripped you out
Of my tender flesh
The blood gushed freely
The pain was intense

But now that you have been removed
The wound begins to heal
The pain recedes
And there is no limit to how far
I can reach

White Lines

I watch the white lines
In my car wing mirror
As they descend rapidly into the distance
The landscape behind me
Begins to fade and disappear

It reminds me of my journey
How I continue to travel
Each white line replaced by another
Stretching out towards the horizon

I have left many things behind
The ups and downs of my past
Distance and time reduces their impact
And I move forwards
And Beyond

Ghosts

The road takes me home
The home of yesterday
Along the way
The ghosts glide in and out
Of my memory

Echoes of the past
I would rather forget
I wonder if/when I stop going 'home'
They will leave me forever?

I have shed that skin
Not a cell remains from that time

I am a different person
Shiny and new

Friendship

A

How sad for you
That your heart is closed
To forgiveness
To kindness
To empathy

It must be a lonely path
You walk

But you and I have reached a fork in the road
And we travel in different directions now

It's very sad
But it's how it must be.

Losing a Friend

Am I losing you?
My friend...forever?

It feels like you're sinking down
Under the debris
Of a life unresolved

Your hands reach out to me
I am your moral compass

You look to me for guidance
That I cannot provide

For your ears are closed
And your heart is too full

And yet
It makes me wonder...who guides me?

At times like this
Of uncertainty
Of questioning

My first instinct is also to reach out
For support
For guidance

But where do I look?

Everywhere I turn
People are a mess

Self-serving
Unforgiving
Closed

I guess I really am alone
On my journey

The Buddhists were right
The only person you can reply on

Is you.

My Friend

Who needs Sat Navs and roadmaps?
Who needs emails and texts?

Our closeness is not defined
By geography or technology

When you are sad or hurt
I cry and hurt with you

When you laugh and jump for joy
I laugh and jump with you

Others have come and gone
But our connection remains
Stronger than ever
Transcending time or miles

My friend
Forever

Friendship

Often, they gently arrive
And become entwined with your life
They travel alongside you
Through the ups and downs
They offer kindness, love and laughter
And a shoulder to lean on

So, when the dial turns again
And time moves along
And we find they are no longer
Weaved into the fabric of our lives
It's sad
We miss them
We grieve

And so, it is for me
I see the many smiling faces
Reflected in the mirrors of my past
They are no longer by my side
But what they have given me remains

Memories. Laughter. Love. Companionship
Mutual support. Someone to turn to
Someone to confide in
They are part of me now
The ripples of their existence
Gently lap over me...forever

I must learn to appreciate
What I have gained
Not to mourn
What I have lost

My journey continues forward
And there are many travellers
Still to meet along the way
And so, I carry on

Emma

Words are inadequate
To describe our friendship

The feeling I have often
Felt with you
Conveys so much more

When my heart was broken
And I felt splintered into tiny pieces
I lost my way
And forgot to care for myself
You were like an anchor
That held me firmly
Your gentle soothing words
Your knowledge of my history
Your lack of judgement
Helped me to find my way back
When I felt lost

I felt over the years
That my pain is your pain
That my sorrow is your sorrow
That my triumph is your triumph

You were with me always
And I with you

Our friendship is the most precious treasure
And I fully appreciate
How rare and valuable it is

Thank you, my friend,
For all that you give me
For all your gentle kindness

You are a very special part
Of my journey

Hurt

The wound of disappointment
Of being let down
Is open again

Is it me?
Are my expectations too high?
Unreasonable?
No, not on this occasion

The gnawing, hollow reality
Is that we are not that close
Not really

Sure, we talk the talk
Buy the presents
Maintain the façade

But do I really know you?
Do you let me see?
You are afraid and my directness
And desire to be closer
Scares you
So, you back away

You can't handle it

Part of you wants it
Sometimes
But you can't sustain it

Ambivalence

I know this
Because I am much the same

But this is just too important
To brush under the carpet
You've let me down
And, right now, I'm deeply hurt
I cannot forgive you

A Valuable Lesson

I'm learning that
Not all relationships
Are meant to last
Forever

Often, they are transitory
Moments in time
Where two people are connected
And, in time, disconnected

We only allow people to see
What we want them to see
We dance around each other
Fleeting moments of intimacy
Followed by
Detachment and loss

I believe everyone
Who enters my life
Has something to teach me
A lesson that I need to learn
To prepare me for my onward journey

And sometimes
It is then time
To move forward
Without them

I greatly value the relationships
I've had in my life
They have helped to
Mould and shape me

But wisdom comes
In knowing when to
Let go

It's important to acknowledge
The sadness and loss
But equally to
Continue the search
For understanding
And meaning

Intimacy

Will You Wait for Me?

You were sent to me
Of that I am sure

To heal the wounds
Of the past

But I fear....
Will you wait for me...?
Until I can truly be with you?

With you I feel secure
For the very first time

When we lie together
Wrapped so tightly around one another

Our toes brushing
Every inch of skin melting together

We are one
Whole again

But when the wounds are open
The gulf between us can feel so vast

Until the next time that we merge
And all is right again

Is it enough for you my love......?
Will you wait for me......?

You and Me

I see in you, a reflection of myself
Sometimes I don't like it
And I don't want to look

But you stay with it
Your arms open to let me in
And keep me safe
Allowing me to feel

Safe in your embrace
I'm able to grow
You nurture me

And when you need me
My arms are open
To scoop you up
And nurture you right back.

Alone

When you're away
I feel so alone

Sure, I get things done
Self-sufficient, that's me
Always had to be

Learnt it as a child
Look out for No.1
Staying silent
Unseen and unheard
A severed connection
From those close to me

Now this distance reverberates
An echo from the past
You may even be in the room
But it feels like you're gone

And then you want to be close
To possess me
This sudden shift
Feels overwhelming

I need to keep a piece of myself
For me
To keep me safe for the next time
You go

Bliss

This moment is pure perfection
The sound of the sea
A gentle hush in the distance
The cool breeze strokes my warm skin
The feel of your strong arm
Wrapped safely around my body
Your warm breath on my neck

My body is floating serenely
Above the tranquillity of this moment
My eyes gently closed and resting
An ecstatic paralysis
Of time and sensation
Utter quietness
We are completely alone
This moment of blissful connection

Here We Are

Here we are
You and I
I feel the intensity of this moment

Like an invisible thread
Binds us together

Our hearts and souls
Connected
Joined
Linked
As one

The birds have stopped singing
The sun has lost its heat
The room has melted into just you
Time has stood still

Intimacy
How intoxicating
It trickles over the senses
Like butter on warm toast

Hold on to it
Savour it
For it won't last

Oh, but what a gift……

Easy to Forget

It's easy to forget
That you were once a little boy
Confused and lost
Tossed around in the storm
Of chaos and uncertainty
That your parents created

It's easy to forget
That those deepest wounds
Never truly heal
The pain may lessen in time
But the scar remains deep

It's easy to forget
That the tall, strong, smiling man
Standing before me
Sometimes feels small and scared
And alone

I will try to remember
That underneath
You and I can be vulnerable
Together

Intimacy

It's in the way you hold my hand
The way you stroke my hair
It's in the way you like to make me laugh
The way you show you care

It's in the way our toes rub together
The way our bodies entwine
It's in the way your arms open up to me
And you tell me it's going to be fine

Time has no meaning in my love for you
Our bond grows as the years go by
The silver in your hair may tell me so
But with you I have learnt how to fly

Imagine our future, far from now
When we've both turned old and grey
Sharing our families' ups and downs
Remembering to laugh all the way

Eleven Years Today

Eleven years ago, today
You walked into my life
With a twinkle in your eye
And a Cheshire cat smile

We talked about everything
And nothing
I don't really remember

But I do remember
The way our smiles met across the room
Like headlights on full beam

Eleven years ago, today
You took my hand for the first time
It was warm and gentle and reassuring
Totally natural

I remember thinking
"This is what I've been waiting for"
My heart began to stir
The ache of loneliness
Began to lessen

I knew we were somewhere beautiful
The lakes and the trees surrounded us
But I didn't notice any of that

We sat and a had a warm drink on a cold day
You sat opposite me and your eyes sought mine
You gently leant forward to kiss me
And oh, what a kiss

It was the kiss I needed so badly
A kiss that touched my soul
A kiss filled with such promise

I remember that day eleven years ago
As if it were yesterday

Tenderness

You wrap your arms tightly around me
And gently kiss my nose
I feel safe
And warm
And loved

Our toes brush together against one another
There's no space between our bodies
As they merge into one

You kiss my head
My eyes
My mouth
My neck

The world around us disappears
There is only this moment
I am totally absorbed
In your loving embrace

Gateway

Soft, white and fleshy
Guardians of the sacred place
Your role was always to protect
But, in doing so
You restricted my passion

Now the energy flows freely
I feel the possibilities
The limitations are behind me
And I soar upwards

The lines of communication
Have reformed
My body has been tuned in
I have taken possession of it once more

The liberation is indescribable
Every movement
Every sensation
Every touch
Every caress
Awakens and stirs me

I am truly alive

Permission

I've opened up
To let you in
Only now
Our hearts are joined
United, as one

It makes me sad to think
How I held you at arm's length
Prevented you
From looking inside me

But I was afraid
Of what you might see
A dark, dirty, shameful place
So, I kept that part locked up

Now I've had the courage
To look for myself
Accept, nurture and love
My pain, my vulnerability

So now I have no reason
To stop you from looking
I want us both to see each other
For who we really are

Connection

There was a time
When I believed
I had to open my legs
To feel connection with a man

To make an impression
On his heart – and his soul
I surrendered my body
But I failed to see
That the barbed wire
Around my heart
Kept me safe
And kept him out

I had to learn
Tenderness
A gentle caress
The warmth of a hand holding mine
The bliss of toes brushing
The ecstasy of hair being stroked

I had to learn
That a man is many things

Have courage, be brave
Open up your heart
And let him in

Released

There's a fire in my belly
Igniting my whole body
No longer cut off
Disconnected

Is this passion?
If so, I've known it before
But it was fleeting and transitory
Now, it sleeps like a gentle flame
Glowing and warm
Waiting to be brought to life

With your touch, you stir me
Our bodies entwined
You hold me safe
And release me
All at the same time

Like a delicate flower
I feel my petals gently unfurl
One by one
Seeking the light and warmth
Of your love

Dad

My Dad

The sweeties on a Saturday
Rainbow puffs and The Chart Show
Every week
A gift, a thought, for your daughter

The trips to see family
Sunday porridge
Growing vegetables in the garden
Spending time together
Gifts to your daughter

Help with the decorating
A willing gardener
A granddad, snuggled up, reading books
Gifts for your grandchildren

You may not see all you've given me
Over the years, dad
But I see it
And I love you for it

Because you're *my* dad.

Letter to Dad

I'm dreaming of writing a letter to dad
To share my heart with him
To bare my soul
To help him to understand
What it's been like to be his daughter

The wound is so great
The prospect is scary
I risk alienating him
I fear rejection

But how long do we have left?
Do I grab the opportunity?

What lies beneath for him?
Does he also wish we were closer?
Does he feel the sadness?
A desire to connect
But not knowing how to......?

Knowing Dad

I want to tell you
How much I love you dad
You have always been there for me
Your quiet presence has guided me
Your reliability helped me feel safe
Your steady influence
Was a solid platform
From which, I launched myself into the world

I would love to know
Your inner thoughts and feelings
I would love to hear
That you love me
You are proud of me
You are interested in my life
You value me as a daughter
That I'm still – and always was – your little princess

I can see you as a little boy
So unsure of yourself
Not really knowing where you belong
Vulnerable and lost
You once told me that your dad
Was never interested in you
Would it hurt you if I told you
I have felt the same
All my life?

I've been searching for you
In my relationships
Within myself
Where are you?
I ask myself "how can I strengthen our connection?"

But now I see clearly
I love you
When I embrace you and you hold me tight
You love me too
I've found what I'm looking for

It was there all along

What it Means to be a Man

A vulnerable little boy
Lost and uncertain
Searching for acknowledgement
Yearning to be loved

He grows up in a world
That teaches him "be strong, don't cry"
He must provide

But what of softness, tenderness?
Does he hear his heart speak?
Can he allow his soul to guide him?
Will this world we live in
Provide him with what he needs?

Or does he swallow it down
His inner thoughts and feelings
This surely makes him a man
Right?

Wrong

To be a man is to be strong, yes
But to be man is also to be tender
To be a man is to nurture the ones you love

To be a human being
Let you heart and soul be your guide

The Enlightened Self

Golden Light

I sit alone
Still and silent

Filled with peace
And love

Above me
A light shines brightly
Bathing me in its glow

The light trickles down
Embracing every part of my being

I am love
I am light
I am peace

The light extends outwards
To those I love
With glowing hands of light
Surrounding my beloved in warm embraces
Connecting us all
As one

Moments

They are what I live for
These moments of being moved
Beyond the everyday
Transported to places surreal and dream-like
Places and feelings that touch the soul and capture the heart
In all its capacity
To see and feel love.
Is this the feeling you can buy in a pill or a bottle?
A euphoric, almost paralysed
Quietness where no words
Are needed or can satisfy
A description of how I'm feeling
It's magical and mysterious
And indescribable
These moments
Are what I live for.

Less is More

Why speak when silence
provides what I need?

Why ponder and question
when others don't have the answers?

Why make others feel comfortable
when my own needs are not met?

Why seek guidance outside
when inside holds the key?

Why keep doing
when, by not doing,
you achieve so much more?

Knowing

How many people
Are fortunate enough
To know
Why they are here?

Who am I?
What's my purpose?
Why am I here?
They ask
Rarely do they find an answer

But I know

My purpose in life is
To heal
To nurture
To reconnect that which has become
Disconnected

We are all in search of The Self
Our souls direct our journey
If we are willing to listen

The Healer

I am an intrepid explorer
I am courageous and strong
A warrior
Unafraid to enter the places
Others keep tightly sealed

My courage liberates others
Beyond my own pain and suffering
I guide those who need to lean on another

Long ago, I may have been known as
A Shaman
A medicine man
A witch!

Among those who share the sight into another world
Of mystery and the unknown

There is fear surrounding darkness
Until we are able to shine a light
Into the corners
And witness what is hidden there

If we dare to look
We may discover an inner wisdom
That sets us free

Wholeness

Light radiates from the centre
An intensity of brilliant light and warmth
The shimmering nuggets of gold
Encapsulate the lightness of spirit
The purity of the soul
The personification of beauty
Of love, kindness, generosity and compassion

Tendrils of liquid gold
Resonate outwards to the surface
And beyond
Affecting everything in their path
The challis that contains
Will not limit their potential

The shadows of the past
Provide perfect contrast
To the brilliance of the light
Allowing that which has been hidden
The opportunity to greet the sun
To be seen
To be acknowledged
To be healed

In this moment, my fears are unravelled
The transformation, the enlightenment
Of recent times
Was it lost amongst the debris of the everyday?

My soul speaks to me and soothes
No, the work is never undone
Go inward, be still, be quiet
All you need is waiting there for you.

Love

A warm, gentle glow
Deep in my inner soul
Radiates pure love
Compassion
And generosity of spirit

It pours outwards
And envelops the ones I love
Opening up our hearts
And connecting us as one

My love extends further
To encompass all humanity
The joys and sorrows
Of all who walk side by side

I see beauty everywhere
The wondrous, awesome
Power of nature
Lifts me to the highest place
Where my spirit soars free

I can acknowledge the shadows
The wounds are part of who I am
But they no longer define me
I have transcended beyond

Finally, I am free

Focus

My focus has shifted
Where once, I would hone in on the dark
I now see mostly light
The dark exists, and I acknowledge it
But it no longer defines my experience

Where once I saw only a victim
I now see a strong, courageous woman

Where once I was pulled towards negativity
Now I repel it with force

I exist in the light
I open up my heart to let it all in

Submerged

I never knew it was possible
To feel such calm
I feel unaffected by the troubles
That surround me
I allow myself to feel my response
And it becomes my experience

Some dark clouds loom
But I do not fear them
I see them as opportunities
To learn, grow, evolve, understand
I will embrace whatever they bring
And continue on my journey

I am submerged in the universe
I feel its effect in every fibre
Of my being
I say hello to the trees, the birds
I am part of it all
I am filled with love, kindness
And hope

Family

Having looked more closely
I can now stand back
And see my family
With new eyes

Home was a warm, safe, steady place
And there was plenty of love
But I didn't always feel it
And once the rupture
Cracked open my soul
Things were spoilt and distorted

But now, looking back
I see that I have re-found myself
The creative, playful, imaginative
Little girl of my early years
Beautiful in every way

The ghosts can be laid to rest
And this opens up new channels
Of love and tenderness
I reconnect and communicate
And express myself

I want to make the most of every day
To wrap my arms around my family
And hold them closer to me
To pour out my love
And feel the warmth of its return

I want to dance and sing
Draw and laugh and explore
I want to write and read and learn
I want to be me, now
Born out of the me
I used to be

Now

I want to capture this time of my life
As I approach my 44th year
I'm aware of a contentedness
That I've never known before

My world gravitates around my family
My children, my animals
And the love of my life
We live in a beautiful place
My work brings meaning and purpose
To those I support
It helps me reaffirm my place
In the wider world

I belong

I don't shy away from the darkness
And sadness that lies at the periphery
Of everyday life
Death, loss, illness, cruelty, war, difficulty
I acknowledge it, and in doing so
I am able to embrace its twin
The Light

For me, the light does not come
In a religious form
It is in the beauty of our natural world
In the faces and laughter of our children
In the playfulness of our animals
In the loving look from those who cherish me

It is in the small acts of kindness
Of every day
The thoughtfulness and care I give to others
And receive back in return

I want for nothing
I am full and complete
How lucky am I?

Not lucky in fact
I have created my life
And worked hard and struggled to get to this point
So now I reap the rewards
I deserve it all

Prayer to The Self

If I listen carefully
To the voice from within
I will be guided
And soothed
Comforted
And acknowledged

If I do not expect this from others
I will not be disappointed

If I have faith
In my own judgement
If I believe
I know what's best
What feels right
I will be wise

If I look for strength
From within
I will be brave
And resourceful
I will not rely on others
To hold me up

If I nourish myself
With kindness
And self-compassion
I will not need to be nurtured
By another

When I am vulnerable
And need comfort, support,
Acknowledgement, guidance,
Strength or kindness
I have faith that
I will know
Where to look
And where not to look

Content

All those years of
Aiming
Progressing
Achieving

Now I find myself
In a place
Of utter contentment
I'm where I want to be
In every sense

That's all I need to say

Serenity

I allow myself to feel
I accept life and all it brings
I trust my love for others
And their love for me

I allow myself to just be
No longer rushing
Or pushing myself
I have everything I need

I am tranquillity
I am serenity

Mum

Forgiveness

Forgiveness is not all encompassing
It's not black or white
It can be murky, mottled and grey

I know you would never intentionally hurt me
or cause me pain
I know that you love me
I know that you want what's best for me
and always have

But....

I *feel* that you still should have known
You still didn't protect me
You failed to *notice*
And that is the part I cannot forgive

So, each time I'm in pain
And you fail to notice
The disappointment re-emerges
And I withdraw from you
So, I don't have to look you in the eye

Because I wouldn't be able to lie
I am hurt
You did fail me
And I can't ease your conscience

I've learnt to trust my intuition
And it tells me I am allowed to feel this way
It's OK

Forgiveness # 2

Driving home
The realisation hits me
I forgive you
It is simple
And pure

I love the person I have become
And she has been born out of
Sadness *and joy*
My experiences have made me
Who I am
I am your daughter
I know you love and cherish me

And that is all I need

I have spent my life
Carrying around shame
Please don't spend the rest of yours
Burdened by guilt

Let us both, let it go

Numb

I don't know how I feel
I'm not sure I feel anything
What will it mean to not have you
In my life?

I don't know
Because it's never happened

You've always been there
Sometimes in the background
Always by my side
And in my heart

I won't know until you're gone
All the things I will miss
But I have an idea
And just the thought of it
Makes me sad

Perhaps that's why I'm numb
I'm not ready to go there yet

Two Magpies

"Two for joy"
So the saying goes
I watch the pair
Playing and chasing one another

I ask myself
"How can there be joy at a time like this?"
You are dying
With each passing day
You grow weaker
And more distant

And yet....

A feeling begins to gently grow
The knowledge that I will be ok
That I have felt responsible
For your happiness
Your wellbeing
For all of my life

Your death will release me
From that burden

Even in the darkest place
There is always light

Ambivalence

I'm feeling so disappointed

Having spent most of my life
Protecting my heart
Only partially letting people in
I learned how to open up
And allow love to pour out

I now find
I'm back in the old familiar groove
Gently closing myself off
Wanting to hide
Feeling exposed

The old wounds are open again

But it's not the same wound
That it always was
The healing that has taken place
Is truly extraordinary

I must be patient
I must give myself permission
To accept
That you were not perfect
And when I was disappointed with you
The barriers would go up
So I could defend myself
Against how much it hurt

Now that you're gone
I wonder, will that ever change?

Eternal

Mum, I will miss so many things
Your hugs and kisses
Our conversations
Sharing
Your touch
Giggles and silliness
Someone to talk to
About life's ups and downs

So, for now, I feel the deep sadness
A deep pit of loss
Throughout my whole being.

But....
I know
That you are – and always will be
With me
You are a part of me
I see you in my love of art and nature
I see you in my children
I see you in my garden
You are everywhere
You are here inside me

And so, your presence
Is eternal

I will make sure you are not forgotten
I will not push down your memory
Turn over the photographs
Because I cannot bear the pain
Of losing you

I will allow myself to feel it
In honour of my love for you

And in time
I hope that the pain will lessen
And the sun will shine again
For all of us
Who loved you

Rest in peace now
My love
The recent dark times
Are behind us all now

Let us all look up into the light
And feel the warmth of the sun
On our skin
And remember you

Forever....

Treasure

My last moments with you
Were more precious
Than any words
Could ever describe

I held your tiny, frail
Hand in mine
Brought it to my face
Just to feel you close

I told you how much
I would miss you
Not sure that you could even
Hear me

But my last words to you
"I love you mum"
Were answered with a whisper
"I love you too"

Index of Poems

Lightning Source UK Ltd.
Milton Keynes UK
UKHW010657040319

338417UK00009B/587/P